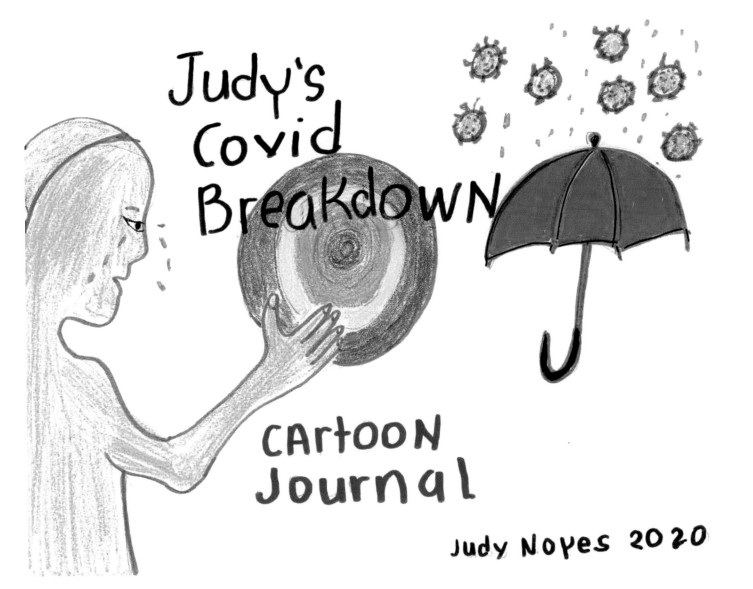

To order additional copies of this book, contact:
Xlibris
844-714-8691
www.Xlibris.com
Orders@Xlibris.com

ISBN: Softcover   978-1-6641-4196-4
      Hardcover   978-1-6641-4197-1
      EBook   978-1-6641-4198-8

Library of Congress Control Number: 2020922371

Print information available on the last page

Rev. date: 11/24/2020

THIS BOOK IS DEDICATED TO MY DAD,
James W. Howard, 1930-2014.

He was an accomplished fine artist and he left behind countless watercolor and printmaking works of art. He drew the following cartoon when I got married in 1995. He would have really gotten a kick out of my creation of Covid-19 Cartoons. He had a wonderful life. He was thankful that he had the opportunity to create art and had many good friends.

I am grateful beyond measure that he and my mom were so committed to exposing me to the arts, music and culture. Peace be with all who enjoy this book.

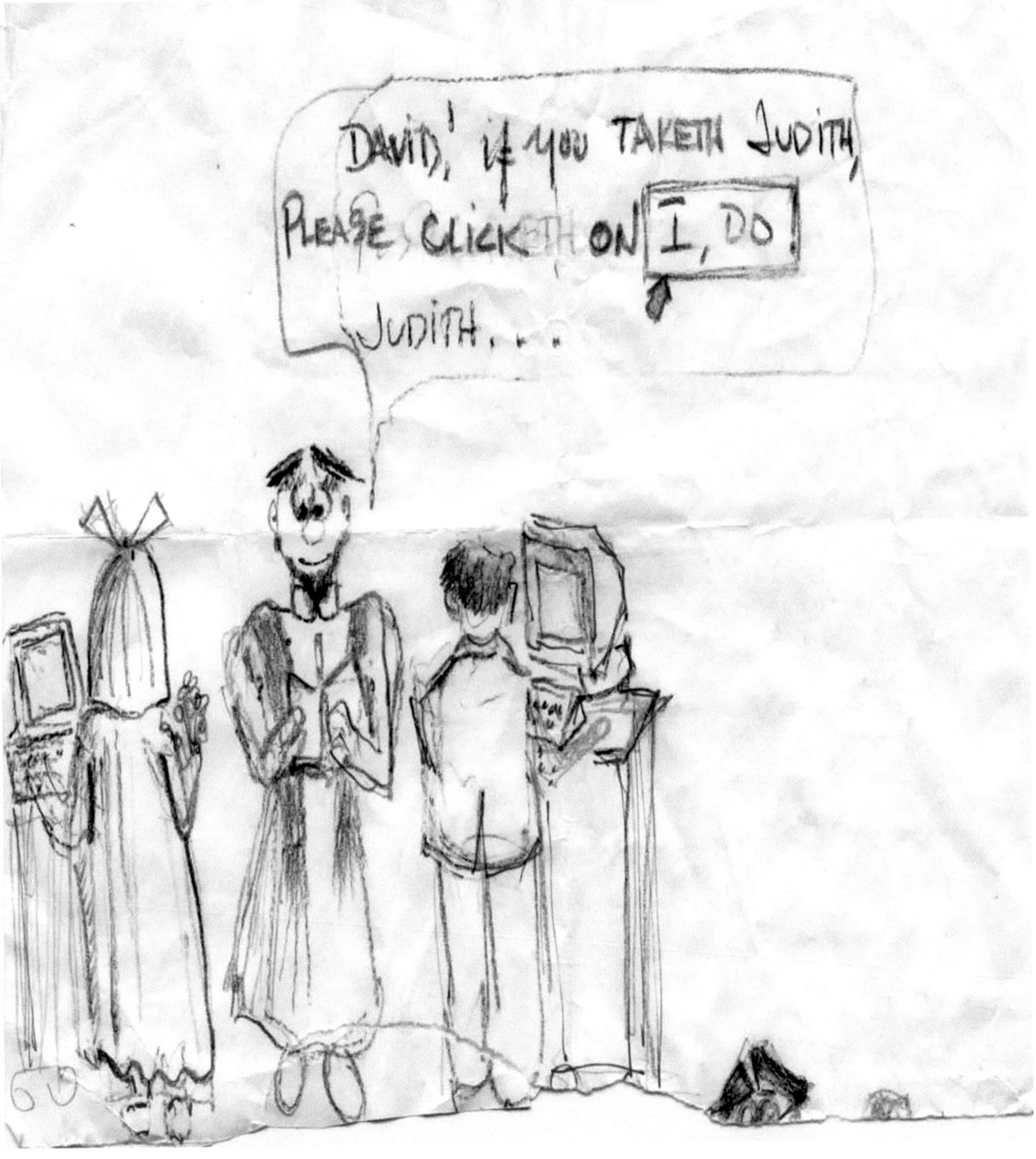
DAVID, if you TAKETH JUDITH,
PLEASE, CLICKETH ON
I, DO
JUDITH. . .

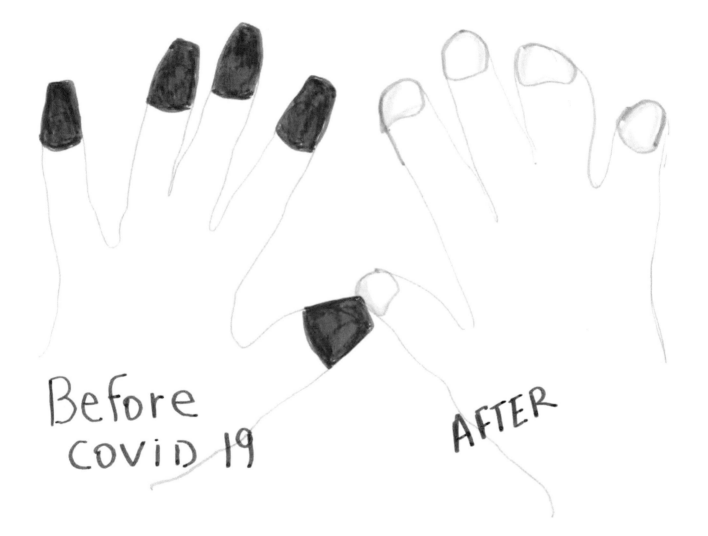

Before covid 19

AFTER

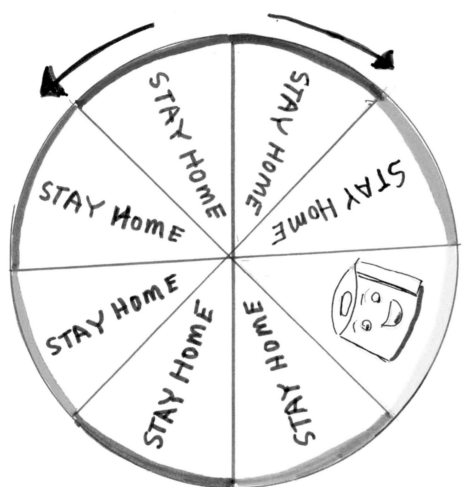

Wheel of Fortune

NOW What are WE AFRAID OF?

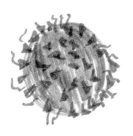

SOCIAL Distancing

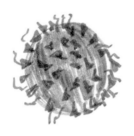

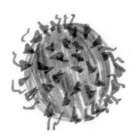

I wanna
Hold Your Hand

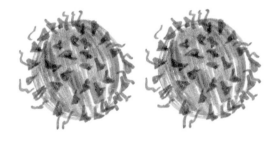

I Get knocked
DOWN, but I Get
up again.

I  Bingo

All The days are Gone

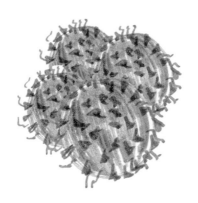

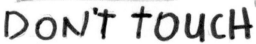

Corona	Corona	Corona	Corona	Corona

Watermelon
Wheat
Sold out

Vanilla Porter
Sold out

coconut
Stout
Sold
out

Peach IPA
Sold out

Summer BREWFEST   Cancelled

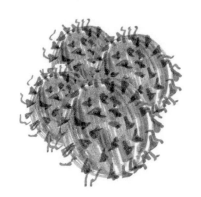

Mother's DAY 2020

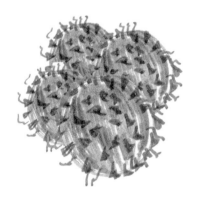

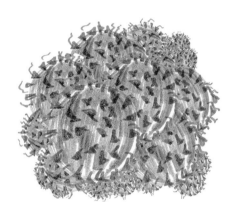

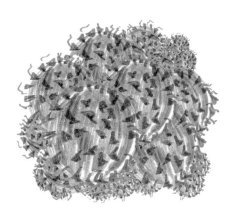

MY
SCREEN
FROZE

Just
CLICK
ON
"I DO"

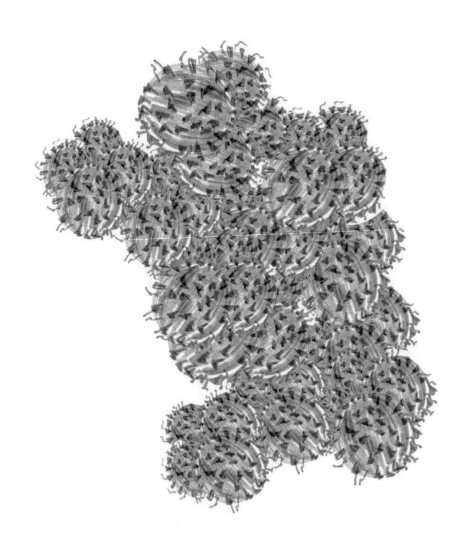

cough cough
Sweeping out the trash
DON'T WORRY. I've been Tested.
June 2020

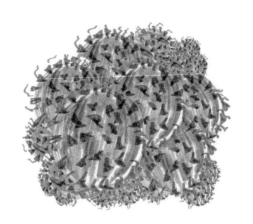

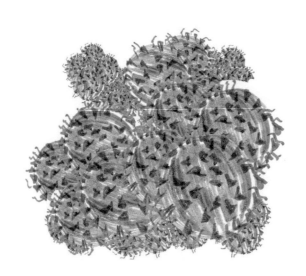

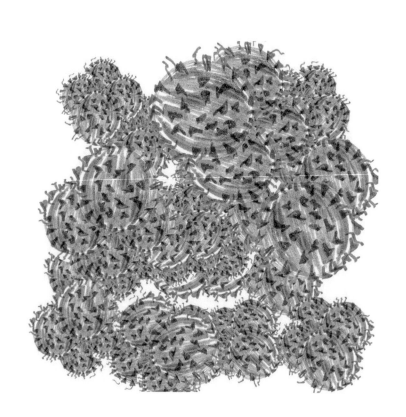

The Magic Kingdom

The happiest Place on earth.

The KOOLAID is Expensive.

Magical Thinking is ALL OK.

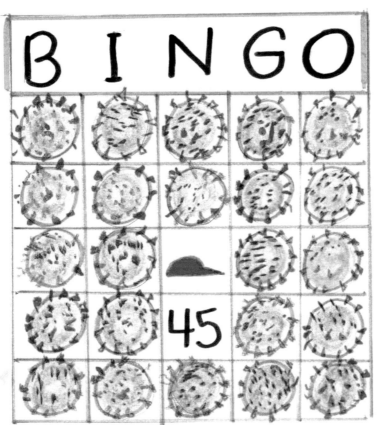

BINGO

This BINGO CARD SUCKS.

Keep Your Face
Toward the sunshine
AND The shadows
Will Fall
Behind You

PLEASE
PLEASE
VOTE

WAlt Whitman
1819 - 1892

JUDITH CAPTURED
THE MOOD AT A LOCAL BLM PROTEST

Printed in the United States
By Bookmasters